WHAT IS THE POINT?

A nobody's guide to life

By Peter Tideswell

Edited By Khaleda Zaman

Text copyright © 2017 Peter Tideswell
All Rights Reserved

Table of Contents

Table of Contents

Prologue

Who are you and where are we?

Living in the moment

Nutrition

Breathe hard

Reps

Importance of failure

Piano and guitar

Switching targets

Prolificacy

Probabilities

Good company

Money

Drug addiction

Religion

Motivation

How to be good

The end

Prologue

This book aims to give you clarity. It is a simple set of thoughts on many of the main issues of modern day living. You may wish to use this book as a tool to question your outlook or as a way of finding a path through life.

No matter who you are, this should set out to you what it takes to live a happy, fulfilled life when maybe you're not feeling like that is possible right now.

I hope to have simplified the subjects and although what I state may not be new to you, it should serve to instil the qualities necessary to succeed. Best of all it won't take long, because of course, your time is precious and there's not a second to lose.

Who are you and where are we?

If you have gotten this far then you need help. You have been battered by the world. Whatever has caused you to look for guidance is something you can be proud of and thankful for.

Those in life who appear to be successful, in whatever way you believe success to be, have one thing in common, they received help. If up-to-now you have fought a lonely war then be proud you've made it this far.

Humans are capable of the most incredible achievements. Look around. Ignore the negatives of society and focus on what years and years of human endeavour has built. Your nearest building didn't make itself. It took cooperation, research, planning, skills, resources and perseverance just to make one tent, one hut, one igloo, one barn, one house, one skyscraper, one space station...

If you believe you don't need or haven't received help, then remove all of the knowledge you have, as this was obtained in a large part through the toils of others before you.

And here is lesson one: accept help. Use the help of others to further your goals. Do not feel guilty for this. Those who help you will gain more pleasure than you will know. The main goal of accepting help should be to use that help for what it was intended.

If it is monetary then put it towards what it is you need it for. If it is knowledge then thank them for their input. It is good practice to write down each and every time you feel someone has helped you.

Lesson two: make notes about everything. Do not do this on a computer. Write everything down and keep records. The act of physically writing stimulates your mind in a way typing cannot replicate. Keep order to your records. As soon as you begin structuring things by pen and paper you will have a clearer mind. Always keep a pen and paper to hand. Your day is filled with interesting important thoughts and moments simply washed away by the next interesting important thought or moment.

Within days you will notice a difference. It is imperative you keep order to your notes, your doodles, and your day to day ideas. From now on you are an employee for a new company. You now work for FutureYou Ltd. Everything you are going to do is to build a better future for you. If the FutureYou Ltd boss won't like what you are doing then you don't do it.

If you have the current mind set of *to hell with the future - live in the moment*, that's not going to cut it. I'll touch on this issue in a bit but for now ask yourself the question, "Where are you?" Here's some help…

Currently you are, I assume, sitting on a huge rock; this rock has about a four mile high dome around it which you can just about live and breathe in. Outside of this is a vacuum; an abyss of virtually nothing. The huge rock you are standing on is moving roughly 66,000 miles per hour through this vacuum around a giant ball of super-heated plasma. This ball is then moving around a supermassive black hole at around 500,000 miles per hour.

Continue moving out and the speeds and distances become more than all of the calculators in the world can handle. The whole entirety of life, the universe and everything in it is ridiculous. It is so shockingly ridiculous most of the human population avoids thinking about it because it is simply too ridiculous.

Humans love to be distracted from the sheer apparent pointlessness of doing anything. We need to be distracted otherwise worldwide insanity would ensue. This planet and this star inhabit a universe which appears to have popped into existence from absolutely nothing. If that doesn't make you want to reach for the drugs then you're a robot and humans are now long gone.

So what is my point? Well, you're screwed. In addition to this, we also know that of all the deaths of all the living organisms since the earth began, there isn't any evidence to show that you can come back. So basically the only thing you have to do in life is nothing. You in fact should do absolutely nothing. Doing nothing is a way of telling the universe: I'm not playing, this game sucks.

Since birth you have been bombarded by the idea that you have to do something; that you have to be someone; that you need to work hard and just get on with living. There's no time to stop and think about what this place is all about, just get on working and you'll be fine. But here you are and you don't feel fine. You've never really made up your mind about what you want to do; you've never really made a choice. Did you ever say, "Yeah, I want to be a bank manager, I want to be a shopkeeper, accountant, village idiot."

Whatever you do to pay the bills, could you look your five year old self in the eye and agree that you are doing what you want to be doing? If yes, then you must be reading this just before you are about to collect your Olympic gold medal and you don't need to continue.

Whatever your philosophy one thing is for certain – you will die someday. It could be at the end of this sentence. It could be on a Tuesday or you may be on Mars trying to harvest potatoes. Whatever way it goes down, this party is ending at some point. And that's what it should be, a party.

You can do nothing; of course you can be frozen by the magnitude of utter pointlessness, but why? Why is that the answer? You are imprisoning yourself. Now that you know the rules of the game, start playing to win. To win is to enjoy your life. Very simply, enjoying your life is winning. You should not be aiming for cheap thrills. You need to aim bigger, you need a quest.

Living in the moment

Living in the moment is a Hollywood dream. Ask yourself where this idea came from? Look around; watch the television, read a magazine. You are being bombarded with this idea to live in the moment.

"Get that car right now! Hey! What do you mean you can't pay now? Who cares, you can have it now and you can pay us back over ten years. Obviously we are going to need more money for you to do that but you won't mind, it's easily affordable."

"Just bought a new car? You're going to need a new look. We have 50% off all clothes right now! That's right 50% off some completely imaginary price. You cannot miss this. Oh wait, what's that? You can't afford it? Okay then maybe you want to think about getting some credit. The first year is 0% interest free on any new purchases, like this brand new watch."

"What's that? You don't want to be tied down to another payment plan on top of the ones you already have? Aaah to hell with that! In a year you'll have paid this off and you'll be much happier right now! Who wouldn't want to be happy right now?"

This goes on and on, holidays, games, nights out, drinking, eating; everything is in your face telling you to have it. An hour on the internet and you won't even know what you have subconsciously been told you have to have. Newspapers, television programs, soap operas and films, they are all against you.

From now on you're going to ask yourself a simple question. When I leave this shop, do I really own this? If the answer is no, then think again, FutureYou Ltd is paying for that. Have you ever gone out and bought things you hadn't intended on buying? They look like nice, shiny, clean products in nice, shiny, clean big branded bags that you bring home, place them on the floor and open.

After you've stacked up the packaging and you're staring down at the products, have you ever had this empty worry inside? This hollow feeling and you know exactly why it's there? From now on you are not going to do that. I recommend avoiding shops altogether until you are in the black. If you can, do your grocery shopping online, budget your main foods and buy fresh when you can. You will indirectly save money this way. You are simplifying a process and removing any potential additional costs.

When you go to pay for your petrol after filling up your car, you are corralled down a hallway of sweets, magazines, chewing gums and special offers. As you already know, this is no accident. But do you truly know how much this subconsciously guides your decisions? Are you 100% confident you are not influenced by any of this? If you don't think so, then you definitely are. You have to know your enemy to defeat your enemy.

Next time you are about to pay for anything, picture an imaginary stereotypical billionaire watching you, just waiting. Here you are spending your hard earned money and there they are getting most of it. Just to be clear, this is not a war between you and "big business". This is you saying I no longer want to spend money that's not mine, paying someone who is already rich, for something I don't need.

When you want to buy something you are going to do it on your terms, with your money. What's more you will feel great about this because you are now in control. By simply questioning every purchase you make you are taking back control. But let's not be naïve, you may suffer from a lapse in concentration. Accept it for what it is. Do not dwell on it. You are not aiming to be perfect. You are aiming to be better. Small positive changes lead to massive positive gains.

Nutrition

The food you eat greatly affects how you behave in the world. You are what you eat is a perfect summary. Here's another, Eat shit, feel like shit. Again, you may not realise it but you've been bombarded with food propaganda your whole life.

In the beginning you had next to no say in what foods went into your body. Your guardians should have fed you what they regarded as a healthy diet so that you could have the best of starts in life. Different guardians have different ideas about what this consists of.

The variation of what to eat is vast and variation is good for humans. As a species we need to have differing diets. If we all ate the same foods then this could easily lead to widespread disaster. The reliance on a small sample of foods has already caused many species of animals to die out and will no doubt lead to more. So a varied diet can only be a good thing, as the Earth's environment is greatly varied and enjoyably so.

Now the issue with food is the science behind it. With the internet at everyone's beck and call it is quite easy to confirm and then dismiss any statement made about diet. The statement I have just made about the benefits of a varied diet will easily have a counter-argument just a click away. How are you supposed to know what's good and bad in a sea of manipulated information? What's more, nutrition has now become quite a sinister world.

As with all commodities, they have a value. If I have a field full of corn, when it is time to sell, I want to get the highest price for it. If I have many cornfields then I want to do the same but more people will help me do so. More fields equal more workers, and more workers' families and all their livelihoods depend on me getting a good price. Now if I own an entire country's output of corn I want to make damn sure that no one can step foot on my corn making empire. I want to make damn sure that there is a demand to go with the supply I've created.

I'm now worth a fortune which means there is another thing I can do. I can now employ people to advertise corn. I can get these same people to tell the world how good corn is. If the world doesn't believe me, then what can I do? I can get these people to lie about how good corn is. I can pay these people to experiment with corn so that these "scientific" experiments tell the world corn is good for you no matter what the actual results are.

But there may be real scientists who scrutinise the experiment. They believe that the experiments were poorly done or the conclusions are deliberately misleading to push an agenda. Ah well, I can pay people to shut those scientists up. Or I can pay people to discredit those scientists. It's quite easy to get people to believe anything when you have riches. These practices have been going on since the dawn of mankind and will inevitably continue, don't be suckered in.

Everyone has a game plan because not everyone wants to be rich but everyone wants to be comfortable. The farmers tending to the corn farm need an income to support their lives. The fear of losing their income means they are now in the corn farm camp. They are cheerleading for the corn industry. They will help spread the corn propaganda as much as the corn farm owner. The larger the business grows, the larger the impact on people. The more people rely on this business, the more the people are willing to turn the other cheek to the negatives of the business. This is normal as everyone has a deep down inbuilt desire to survive. Now replace corn with anything and you can see how this system creates a world that rewards having money and gives scant regard for anything else.

What is true for most organisms is true for human kind too. The population craves balance. There are opposing forces and they fight towards equilibrium whether they know about it or not. There are those on the planet that see major issues and speak out about them to try and change things for what they see as the better. They behave differently in the hope others will follow and thereby applying extra weight to one side.

It feels like now we don't have a balance. The man in the high tower has only got to pay the right people and any bad practice can continue. Even if it will wipe us all out it doesn't matter so long as the money keeps rolling in. This may seem like a modern problem but this has been going on since day one. Only now the power that the few possess is far greater and far more damaging, as there is nowhere to avoid the results of these dealings.

Food though, food is your fuel. And food is pretty simple for the everyman. Vegetables; it's that simple. Wash them, cook them as little as possible and eat them. Eat them all. Don't add sauces, garnishes or anything additional. Eat them as close as you can to them coming out of the ground. They are rocket fuel. By all means eat meats, carbohydrates, sugars and anything else you want but always aim for at least three quarters of your daily intake of food to be a vegetable.

Within days you'll crave them. You'll look forward to eating them. It'll be easy. Your body will change; everything in your body will work better. The thing is, you already knew this. People don't eat veg because they have tuned their senses to want foods that are slowing them down. Mentally and physically the mainstream foods are full of all kinds of things we just don't need and our body has either got to get rid of them or store them. Make it easy on yourself, ignore the propaganda. Be smug that you are tuned in to what's really happening. Don't preach to those not converted, just don't even talk about it.

Lesson three: don't talk about what you are doing. Talk will get you fake praise. It'll get you an early buzz, which will ruin your future goals. The best thing you can do is keep quiet about whatever you are doing. Keep it internal. It's your little secret. You are a secret superhero and this is your origin story.

Don't be rude if anyone asks what's happening with you. Why are you changing your ways? They'll demand to know exactly what you're doing differently and why; because it's interesting. You'd probably do the same. Just say that you are trying something out. Don't go any further than that. If that's not enough for them just tell them you don't want to talk about it. Don't give them some greater than you rubbish, or the "Oh you should be doing this not that". No, you are not here to change them; you're here to change who you are.

If you do a good job then they'll naturally want to copy you but avoid trying to change other people as well as yourself. Making big changes to your life is not something you should do with other people or in competition with other people. This always ends badly. Either one of you falls off the wagon and eventually drags the other down. Or one of you is really good at it and causes the other to resent them. It never ends well.

Don't share what you are doing with your family or friends or say anything beyond: "I'm trying something different". In this case, talking about it is not a good idea. Get on with making changes and enjoy your personal challenge.

Changing your diet is a challenge. But the benefits are huge. Sugar is everywhere. I don't mention fruits for a reason. Sugar is dangerous to you because it's hidden everywhere and you don't really need much of it. Unless you are training to be an athlete you do not need to look into nutrition beyond massive amounts of vegetables. Ask yourself this simple question. Have you ever met an obese vegan? Not going to happen. Eat right and your body wants to move. Your mind feels clear. You can cope with stresses better. Keep it simple and then build from there. Don't look for excuses why this isn't a good idea. Because like anything to do with food you will find them.

Remember that if I don't sell vegetables, I don't want you eating them. I want you to eat what I'm selling. Beware the advertiser.

A high vegetable diet is an incredibly simple way of making your life massively better. They are cheap, quick to prepare and in time, delicious.

Breathe hard

One immediate enhancement to your life can be easily gained through exercise. The amount of improvements to your wellbeing cannot be understated from just a small amount of regular exercise. I am not talking about a major gym session, a marathon or something equally ridiculous. Just one key goal needs to be achieved. You need to get out of breath. One short full pelt sprint per week could change your entire physical make-up.

It's very easy to go against the grain in life. We all have a rebellious side and many learn to rebel against physical activity because of childhood traumas or poor guardianship. What you have to ask yourself is why are you not doing this? Why have you turned your back on something so simple and effective? If you are rebelling against exercise then you are only damaging yourself. You are not proving anything to anyone by not doing it. As with a healthy diet the only person that suffers by not complying is you. If you are rebelling against someone who advocates this lifestyle then you still lose. Something so positive needs to have a place in your life and exercise and a good diet are the simplest and quickest route to feeling great about being you.

Reps

So you want to do something, anything. You want to obtain a new skill, you want to be better at small talk, be stronger, play a musical instrument or be happier? Just anything! You want to do something? Well reps, reps reps. Reps reps reps reps reps.

Repetitions created you. You can walk because you repeated the process time and time again. You corrected, you were corrected, and you changed and then repeated. You did this so much that now you don't even slightly think about this process. This is not an easy process. If you have a child or have seen someone grow up, this is not an easy skill to pick up. It takes around two years. Think about that. Some animals walk and run minutes after birth. Humans do not.

Our care-givers should have mostly done this through encouragement; encouragement to repeat a process again and again. Your guardian should have been able to correct any issues because by their age they should be pretty good at walking. Even without help, babies will learn to walk through observation and process repetition.

Please accept my apology if you do not have legs or you cannot walk but replace walk with chewing, talking, crawling, potty training, you name it the process is the same. Here's where this affects you.

Surprise, surprise you've been brainwashed again. There is not much the average person is not capable of doing. There is a perpetuated myth that a great multitude of people have bought into; that some people are just born better. It's a really good excuse. We worship people who can do seemingly amazing things: musicians, writers, athletes, scientific athletes; whatever. Especially in the western world we are brought up surrounded by media super-heroes. This is carried through by our newspapers, television shows, movies and social media because it's interesting. It's exciting to know that there are people out there capable of awe inspiring greatness. It's entertaining. It's a massive industry churning out huge sums of money to deify people and it's a really good tool to give people dreams. "Look what they can do, wouldn't you like to do that too?"

Well you can't. There are a lot of people walking around that I'd class as dream killers. They'd say that they are pragmatists. "Not everyone can be an Olympic athlete"; "The world needs plumbers just as much as it needs A-list actors."

Yes of course that's true but we need both. We need a lot more plumbers than actors, that's true but this does not mean that when you are a plumber you stay a plumber. That's your lot, you're now a plumber, don't you dare dream about being something else because who's going to fix my drain then? No, you're a plumber so be happy and be the best plumber you can be because not everyone can cure cancer. If you hear similar rhetoric, use it as your fuel.

A lot of people lose sight of their dreams. They become bitter about what they can no longer do. They think the world is a young person's game and are now just angrily stewing until their inevitable bitter death. And what better way to go down with the ship than to take as many people with them as possible.

In an abstract sense I don't blame anyone for anything they do. I don't believe anyone is born a certain way. I think we are heavily defined by our environment and there tends to be a logical reason why people behave in certain ways. Health issues aside you can achieve great things through discipline, structure and the right guidance.

Today, more than any time in the entire history of the planet is the greatest time to be alive. If you can gain access to the internet, wherever you are, you have the tools to evolve and remove yourself from your environment. When someone is good at something it looks easy. It looks damn easy, that's why it's entertaining. When you see someone able to do something well, you become transfixed. We turn these people into gods. And then we use the most annoyingly weak word "talent".

It is a disgusting, overused word. The very idea of the word does nothing but destroy. The definition of the word is "natural aptitude or skill". Just think about what that means. It means buddy, you can't do anything like this because you weren't born with this special ability. Right away I'm better because of my genetics. You can never reach these levels because genetics. Give up, don't bother it is talent.

What the word really kills is achievement. And a lot of the time the revered person encourages this. If everywhere you go you are treated like a god then by golly you'll just pretend you are one. You wouldn't want to bring the curtain down would you?

As soon as people know how a trick is accomplished they lose interest. They no longer believe you to be a god and as such they no longer want you in their lives as much. By revealing how they acquired their skill, they become a normal human instead of a super human. It's actually beneficial for your career to not reveal the secrets of your success until you are satisfied with your lot. And on the subject of that, read anyone who's done anything's autobiography.

It's not difficult. I did this and this happened. I wanted to be a body-builder so I began lifting weights. I wanted to be a painter so I began to paint. I wanted to run a marathon so I started running. It's very simple; if you want to do something then you have to start doing it.

From there comes the questions, "But what do I do here? What should I do there?" We all want the end product today. The impatience of civilization has led to apathy for many. If I can't do that by the end of the day or by the end of the week, then it's not worth it. It'll take too long and it's not going to pay the bills so I just won't do anything. I like the idea of being a writer but I'd have to read a lot and then write a lot and I just don't have the time and it wouldn't be worth it and I don't feel like it today. If this sounds like you then you are not alone.

There are few people in the world with an endless drive to pursue their goals, that's why they are so revered. The secret to success is just doing, little by little, doing. What stops most people is the beginning. If you have ever started to ride a bike in 5th gear then this is what the beginning feels like. We overreach and want to get to the speed fast. But this involves a huge effort just moving the pedals a bit.

We want it now because we live for today. We live in the moment so you just haven't got time to "waste time". If it won't make you money now then it's not worth it. But then following this idea you then slump on the couch, watch a movie, watch some internet videos of other people doing the things you want to do. Whatever you do to "relax" isn't helping. You don't need to relax after a day at work. This idea will kill your dreams.

What a lot of people suffer from is just a simple case of poor planning. You come home from work you've got to do A, B and C and when it comes to doing the thing you really want to do, D, you're too tired. Well straight up D is hiding behind an imaginary wall. D is what you need to do just as much as A, B and C. D needs to be done every day because D is now what you work to do. D can be anything: a physical activity, a hobby, learning something new. You need D to be something that you can get better at. The best thing D can be is a project.

Choose something you've always wanted to do but thought it to be too complicated, too far reaching but something that you will feel proud to accomplish. Pride is obtained by completing the project, not from the attention or praise you may receive from other people. Choose something you've always wanted to accomplish and make that choice quick. This first choice is not set in stone. This is just you deciding that I'm going to try and ride the bike now and wait no longer.

Now how do you do this? How do you go from deciding to do something towards doing that very thing? You look to someone who's nearly or already done it. This is what everyone who's ever completed something great did. You find out how they did it. What did they do? What did they study? If you are fortunate enough to be able to, you ask them. You take notes.

The planning begins straight away. You need to break down what you are trying to achieve into increasingly smaller and smaller blocks; the smaller the better. Break the project down and work back right to day one. Day one needs to be an incredibly easy task; something as simple as cleaning a workspace. The simpler the better because once you have completed day one, the pedals are turning. By cleaning a workspace you are actively moving towards your goal. This day one task needs to be simple because it's a sign to yourself that you are starting. From here on you don't need to do excesses of work on your project. But what you do need to do is a tiny bit of work every day. No matter how small, you need to do something.

As I've said, the more you break down a problem into smaller problems the more a gargantuan task seems minor. Do not set yourself a date for total project completion or dates for achieving goals that are way off. By making the tasks small and achievable then you'll gain momentum.

Lesson four: do not overreach. By setting unrealistically timed goals you set yourself up for failure. If you want to be a surgeon don't give yourself a deadline for achievement. Otherwise, instead of failure being a learning process it becomes a stick to beat yourself with. This can cause major issues because you start to forget why you wanted to do the thing you are beating yourself up for failing to do. Small victories are what we want and when do we want them? However long it takes.

Importance of failure

Everyone loses. No one who has done anything worthwhile did it without failing along the way. The more successful the person the more they will have failed. Doing anything great is a war of attrition. The secret here is that those that are successful just kept on getting up. They kept on trying. They looked at why they tripped and aimed not to trip again. They analysed why someone else could do something better than they could and they vowed to do the same but better. Failing is good but only if you know why it's happening.

I think too many people demand too much from themselves too soon, to the point where they stop. They beat themselves up about losing to the point where they give up. All that they had worked towards is left behind and they move on believing that they were just not good enough. Those who succeed didn't stop at that point. For whatever reason - maybe they had a good mentor to help pick them up - they carried on. And day by day they got slightly better, ever so slightly better until that slip was a long lost memory that fuelled their current success.

If you feel like you may have stopped because you thought you were just not good enough then fear not, that, right there, is failure. It's just taken you a bit longer to realise that that's all it was and not an immovable part of who you are.

Piano and guitar

When I was around 14 years old I began on a quest to learn to play the guitar. I was in a large part, inspired by the scene in the film Back to the Future where Michael J Fox plays Chuck Berry's song, Johnny B Goode. I really wanted to do this so I asked my father for an electric guitar for my 15th birthday and luckily for me, he and my mother obliged. From there on I was on my own. I read books, watched others play live and best of all watched VHS tapes of performances. They had the advantage of me being able to pause the footage so I could see exactly what was going on.

I loved playing and at this point in my life I had a lot of spare time to dedicate to this passion. I'd sometimes practice all through the night and destroy any sleep pattern I had but still feel great because I loved what I was doing. I think my only end goal was to learn to play Johnny B Goode like Michael J Fox appeared to do.

Within not too long I could play a-just-about discernible version of the song so me and my friends started a band and began to write our own songs. Yadda yadda yadda much fun was had, many shows were played and it was a great life experience. There was not a monetary goal to doing any of that, in fact for the entirety of my career as a musician I have received £10, which was then used to pay for a taxi home after the show. It was something I had wanted to do and to this day still do and wouldn't change at all.

Not long ago, two close friends of mine argued with me that playing the piano was a much harder feat to accomplish than playing the guitar. Their point was that when playing the piano both of your hands are playing separate rhythms, which is an incredibly hard skill to conquer. Naturally I was firmly in the guitar camp and had very minimal experience with a piano. I understood their point that playing the piano is a lot like patting your head and at the same time rubbing your stomach.

I then obtained a small keyboard and began to see how hard it really was. I found a complicated song but one with a lot of tutorials. With the internet as my companion I searched through video lessons finding those that were right for me, no VHS necessary. I then for a week, regimentally copied the left handed patterns and then did the same with the right hand and finally I blended the two. I had only learned about a minute of the actual song but I wanted to see what happened to my mind. Funnily enough I realised that the same thing happened as when playing the guitar. My mind adapted to the new tasks just like it did with the guitar. By breaking down the actual motions into their most simple actions I made fast progress.

As with anything, if you do it enough your brain reinforces this routine. It strengthens the message until it is able to be fired off and performed at a lightning speed. Then you do it for your other hand. You practice this again and again and then these patterns can be fired off routinely with no problems and minimal fuss. Now when you go to play them together at the same time it's a lot easier than when you started. I finally filmed my hands to see what they were doing and it was mind blowing how autonomous they appeared. In fact here's the next lesson. Lesson five: analyse your performance.

This is fairly simple; make sure you can see where you can improve. You have to be like the terminator when reviewing what you have done. You need to take time out to see how well you are doing and what you can do to change this for the future. Small details can save you hours.

When reading a recipe or tutorial I like detail. I like to read a bit more about the process than just robotic instructions. If the recipe tells me to beat some eggs then I'll beat some eggs. But if the recipe tells me to beat some eggs with a fork because in the authors experience the fork works best, then I'll now feel like I'm making progress. Insider knowledge is key and it's when people refine a skill that's where the value comes from. I have no idea if the fork is best but at some time someone showed me and it was better than how I was doing it so I carried on doing it.

Okay so back to the piano. When I quickly tried to learn this piano tune I suddenly wanted to do other things. I felt like I was sharper in every aspect. I felt like I had more ideas, maybe not always good ideas but ideas about things I wanted to do. When I slept, I slept well. By learning something new I felt reinvigorated to work at projects I'd put aside and I was able to look at them in a new light. So here's the next lesson. Lesson six: continue to learn.

Switching targets

Learning anything new physically changes your brain. After the initial frantic phase there'll be a period of rest where you may be drawn towards rewarding yourself, this may manifest itself into bad habits or blow-outs. Try to make that period as small as you can. I've spoken about how you can fall into familiar traps and relapse into a former state. This is natural. You need to recognise it and get out of there quick as it does not serve your future self. Again, do not beat yourself up about this, this is natural and it is something you need to work on as with anything in life.

Childhood can be predominantly geared towards action - reward. If you do something good, then you can have this. You need to learn to control what the reward is. What do you want as an outcome? Try and limit the reward to just the completion of what you achieved. Eventually by eradicating this idea of action followed by reward you can gain control of your behaviour and blow-outs won't happen. You'll then feel content by the work you've completed and you won't require a "treat".

A great way to get the momentum back is to switch targets. Create a new project and find another thing new that you can get better at. Something like learning a card trick, or spinning a pen. Something physical is your aim. You're looking for something repetitive, almost trance like.

Doing something simple that you can consistently get better at is healthy. This doesn't have to be physically exhausting. There is a sea of free tutorials out there, watch anything because your aim is to keep learning. Just in the same way your appetite for food changes, so does your appetite for new skills and new knowledge. If you don't feed it then it may switch to something that won't help you.

If you have become stuck on a project, mix things up; you'll be amazed at how two things seemingly unconnected can create a connection, which lead to new ideas and solutions. Now here's another secret of success. Lesson seven: be prolific.

Prolificacy

This means what it says. Do as many different things as you can. If you want to paint then paint, paint lots, try new techniques and merge the techniques but paint many pictures. If you can't afford to paint, then draw, if you can't afford to draw then sit in a room and look at how the light affects the room's objects.

You can always do something towards your goal and it doesn't need to be expensive. Here's another often overlooked point. You, right now, are a better artist than Picasso was. There was a point in Picasso's life when he was drawing stick figures. Even more so there was a point when he couldn't pick up a pencil. No one recorded all the rubbish picture doodles that Picasso did because no one knew what Picasso was going to be capable of, not even Picasso.

Take Lionel Messi, considered the greatest football/soccer player of all time. If you don't know him watch a video of his greatest goals, it's long and superhuman. At some point in both of their lives, my grandmother was more skilled at football than him. This is a fact. At some point he could not run or kick a ball. At some point my grandmother could.

Your potential can only be reached by doing; by failing again and again but with the view to correcting yourself. These things do not happen overnight. You are not special. Society might one day regard you as this. But until you start trying you won't even regard yourself as special. A lot of humanity's greatest inventors, musicians, writers, entrepreneurs, artists, world leaders, you name it, they all did a lot of different varying things before they became the people you may believe they always were.

Perfection is not achievable. It's unreachable just like infinity. You cannot reach perfection or infinity because the very concept would cease to exist. I've repeated myself at varying points and you might be frustrated with this but it is to serve a purpose. Do a lot and you will achieve a lot.

Probabilities

When you woke up today there was a value in existence. This value varies but since you were born it's always been there. This value represents the probability that today you will enter a lift and break wind. That's right, it exists.
If you woke up and made that the aim of your day the probability might be higher than the day before. If you had never even seen a lift or lifts hadn't been invented yet, a probability would still exist but the chance of this happening would be very low but never zero.

This is the universe my friends. As long as the universe is there, then you can't escape probabilities. What you can do is make them work for you. If I don't want to get hit by a car then I should avoid cars. By avoiding cars I am making the probability of me being hit by a car go down. If I want to build my own house and I read a book about building my own house, the probability of me building my own house goes up. If I find a forum where I discuss how other people went about building their own house and I read their thoughts, then the probability increases again and so on. Eventually, it becomes so probable that I would build a house, that I build a house. My family are then happy and the universe is happy because it scratched that itch and that high probability became a certainty.

Gambling harnesses the power of probabilities and manipulates them to achieve an advantage. Lesson eight: keep your money; gambling is not a worthwhile pursuit.

The lottery in my country has 14'000'000 possible winning combinations. If one person was allocated to each combination and stood either side of each other, the line of people would be roughly 4000 miles long. Make probabilities work for you; don't pay for the opportunity to stand in that line.

The house always wins is a famous saying and it is nearly always true. Book-keeping is a mathematical art form. When a bookmaker accepts a bet, they manipulate the odds and accept other bets so that they cover any of their losses. A good bookmaker will manipulate the market they are offering to the point that it doesn't matter what the outcome is, they will always make money. Being the bookmaker or the casino owner is the only sure way of making money, and you still have to be a competent one.

Gambling should be a rarity in your life. For success, you need to minimise uncertainty. You need to know that if I do A B and C then D is incredibly likely to happen. By gambling, you're slowing your journey to success. There will always be people who have made money from gambling. That is probabilities in action but the more they gamble the closer they will come to being bust.

You can't avoid the numbers. You are in a pool of 7,500,000,000 people. If you were to cover each possible lottery combination and repeat it till everyone in the world had a ticket, there would be a grand total of only 535 winning people. It's not worth your time.

Here's a big one. Every day that you wake up, the probability of you dying that day is slightly greater than it was the day before, until the day you don't wake up. The clock is ticking, don't waste it with uncertainties.

Good company

Surround yourself with the right type of people. A key issue which might be a little unsettling is that your family and friends may be a hindrance. This is solely about your goals. These people are those you love the most. They may have sacrificed so much for you up-to-now and you owe them. What you do not owe them is devout worship. These people are as fallible as the next. You are these people.

Each and every one of us is the star in our own feature film. For the most part we do what we believe to be the best thing for a given situation. However well-intentioned, once the dust has settled this may not be the best course of action but at the time it felt right.

These people guide us and we guide them. But for the things you may want to achieve, their guidance or critique could slow you down. For obvious reasons, criticism from family members and friends will hit you harder than from any other source. Critique of the work you have done will most likely not be helpful because praise will make you sceptical and criticism will make you angry. Separating worthwhile feedback from family and friends can be too much effort and sometimes it can lead you to stop all together. When looking for valuable feedback you ideally want to remain anonymous. If you really want to know what the world thinks of what you have done you have to separate yourself from the project.

What I mean by good company is to be around people who want to achieve similar goals to you. As a group you will encourage each other and you will have more minds dedicated to any problem you have. These minds will be tuned into specific areas of problem solving. This can create a healthy competitive environment. Obviously you need to take care about how involved you get and I am not in the slightest way saying leave your family. The internet is a great way to be a part of a community of people working towards similar goals but whilst still retaining your anonymity.

Money

The root of all evil! The eventual downfall of civilisation. Filthy lucre. Whatever your thoughts on money, you have been forced into playing by its rules. I cannot think of a life you could lead that wouldn't be at some point affected by money. You need money and if you want to live in peace, it's best to have a lot of it.

At the most basic level, how to win this game is easy. I have a set amount of income that's paid to me monthly in exchange for my skills. By the time this income is paid to me again, I need to have not used up the previous months income. To win the game I need to leave a portion of every monthly income and pile it up somewhere safe. I repeat this process until the pile is large enough to cover my expenses for my remaining years and I've won.

If this is so easy, then why does a large proportion of the planet live in debt and squalor? Greed! It's greed on both parties.

The worker wants more and the lender wants more.

You need to learn to control your greed. If you don't think you are greedy then you're deluded. You are programmed this way. Now the level of greed can be minute but it still exists within you. If you don't think you are greedy then go without food for a week and take yourself to a buffet. Greed makes sense for survival. It's a plan to reduce future damage from potential catastrophes. Eating more than you need is good because when the food runs out; you have reserves and can survive longer.

At some point people became so comfortable that their greed became limitless and society encouraged them to keep taking more, to the point where they endangered others. This had been a localized issue for the planet for millions of years but recently things have stepped up a gear. We now have the ability to see the suffering of others on the planet and the impact our greed has on them and yet this doesn't stop us. It further fuels and snowballs and continues to drive civilization towards either complete capitulation or to be a multiple planet organism.

You need to ask yourself where do you fit in? How much is enough for you? Will your pot ever be full enough? Whatever you think, you need to get to the first stage and that is of having a pot and you need to do it fast.

Until you begin to have money you can't make real money. Debts need to be your priority. If you have loans, cards, mortgages do not stick to your monthly repayments. If you can, pay more than needed. Sell things, pick up pennies from the floor and get rid of that cloud hovering above you. The lenders have all the power in this relationship.

When I was growing up I wasn't taught about controlling my finances and never looked to learn myself. I was greedy and ridiculously poor at keeping to a budget. At school I was fed down a road towards going to university. If you didn't have savings already, you'd have to pay for that privilege by taking a student loan. What's more you needed a bank account to have a student loan.

Now when you get the bank account you have to have the student package. This basically meant you get a couple of incentive vouchers, a new account and most important of all an overdraft. This kind of credit facility is brutal. If you don't know, it's a safety net for when you don't have enough money in your account. The bank will let you use their money in the form of an informal loan to an agreed amount. So the trap is now set. If you ever decide to use this facility you better pay it back quickly because it is charged at the highest rate of interest of any form of lending.

What's more is that the bank has the ability to call this informal loan in at any time. This can be a day after you've used it or ten years. They are in charge. This was a mentality back then and if you just Forrest Gump'd your way into this situation you were now in the banks pocket.

My naivety makes me cringe. I believed that no matter what I owed at some point I would be able to pay it off without a problem. Either

I'd be a millionaire, billionaire or my inherent genius would solve the problem. It did but I wasted a long time finding the solution.

Lesson nine: discipline. The word conjures up the idea of doing what you are told and with that comes inevitable rebellion. What is necessary for success is to take your own orders but these orders need to be well thought out. There are a lot of benefits from having a spontaneous side to your personality, but this should never come at the cost of your long term happiness.

Discipline is about having a well thought out structure to your days with an end goal in mind. You stick to that structure and long term credible gains will come. Stick to a well thought out plan and it's inevitable.

Drug addiction

There are many things we need to survive. Our psychology places greater emphasis on certain things than others. Technology may change things, but of the things we need to survive, drugs can turn up and rear their head for longer than we may like them to. They can trick us into believing we need them to survive, but did we ever need them?

I'm using drugs as a blanket term for anything outside of natural foods and water and I want to specifically be vague on this topic. Drugs can do amazing things to us but excess of anything for too long is never beneficial.

Drugs can cause serious life issues that can greatly affect your mortality so they require serious solutions and a serious conversation around them. I cannot provide this for you and it would be wrong to do so or make light of these problems.

There is help out there and if you feel you cannot stop doing what you are doing then understand it and start looking for the right type of help.

There are two problems to face with addiction, first the physical connection and then the psychological. I also want you to understand that there have been many, many people who at one time have been addicted to some of the strongest poisons and through help they have been freed from both connections and have lived happy fulfilled lives after. Treat your problems with respect, gain knowledge of the best solutions and you will overcome.

Religion

Where to start with this one! There are many forms of religion on the planet promoting devout worship to a higher power or worship to a beneficial life structure. Each has a different take on how we should behave and why. Humans need groups and this is something you can't escape. Safety in numbers is the driving force behind this and being an island is a risky survival strategy.

Now, at the heart of the major religions should be the idea of betterment of yourself and your fellow human. If your religion doesn't encourage the two then I'd strongly question why that is and why are you a follower. As a basis of a religion it should be about finding happiness for all and culturing a deeper understanding of why we are here.

In our modern world it is truly amazing that religions have any "good guys" left. I wonder why the "good guys" hang around as the negative actions of the few seem to dominate any religious discussion or newspaper headline.

The manipulation of religious followers throughout history to this day, all for an individual or organization's greed, leaves a sour taste in the mouth. You need to ask yourself, is this right for me? Do I want to continue to be associated with these negatives? I think if you truly believe in the positive message of your religion then it needs you now more than ever.

As with all groups, there are different interpretations and leadership squabbles but with a true religion this should never be the case. The fundamentals of a religion should have been settled a long time ago. Any trumpeted new changes come from literal text interpretations and not the messages they were trying to promote. Times change, new laws come into power for new technologies but our moral compass should be set in stone and laws should be built on these principles.

If you follow a doctrine based on fear then you need to ask yourself, what are you being fearful of? Is it right to only do good in the world because you fear punishment for not doing so? Does this mean that if you were never to be punished for bad actions, you would not do good deeds?

Religion will always have its place in society and I can only hope that the good work it can achieve will not be eclipsed by the misguided few. If you feel you belong to a religious group then do it to create a positive change in the world. Question the morals of your actions at every turn and always remember, hurting someone physically or psychologically has never been the aim of a truly righteous religion.

Motivation

What are you doing this for? This can be a major stumbling block. What will get you to put the hours in? What is going to keep you moving forward? I struggled with this as I never really wanted money. My father was a firefighter and my mother a nurse and we never visibly struggled. We were never well off but we weren't poor, we were comfortable. As a child this environment doesn't give you a sense of urgency. It does give you time to think, but 'what do I want to do?' didn't really get answered because the options were many.

There are vast swathes of the world living in severe poverty or living in places of civil unrest. Survival is their motivation. They have no choice, their options are limited. They act, or they perish. I don't think anyone would like to rely on this type of motivation or ever want to be in that position. But what we can take from this is the urgency and importance of making decisions. You need to make a decision fast. Tell yourself this is what I'm going to do and set out your plan as previously discussed. If you are lacking conviction, just remember that this is not set in stone, this is the beginning. Without an initial decision you will never get going.

For me I finally realised what would really motivate me, freedom. Freedom to go where I want, eat what I want, wake up when I want and work when I want. I know that to obtain this I needed wealth. So every time I think I'd rather sit in front of the television for the evening, I tell myself that I'm standing still. The smallest bit of work will get me close to this freedom but without any I will never move.

Lesson ten: find your motivation and find it fast. Picture yourself living in that future scenario and make the first steps towards it. I guarantee the path to your happiness will meander through places seemingly disconnected and strange, but for your own sake, choose a path and decide on something that will help you stay on it.

How to be good

Well what is good? I suggest good is helping those less fortunate. Helping them to obtain the skills that will lead them to be self-sufficient and then eventually together, we can help the next generation. We all have a selfish streak within us. Without this we have no subconscious motivation to survive. If we accept that, then we can learn how to make this selfishness beneficial for all.

The world has now morphed into a complexly competitive global market and wealth is the key driver. To make important moral societal changes, capital is a necessity. You need funds to change the world, let's not be naïve here. Without money your voice may never be heard so join the game.

The more major world players there are with a social conscience, then the more chance of beneficial social change. We can all make small contributions to creating a better world, but unrestrained greed cannot survive without a balance. It is to the benefit of the rich few, to increase the wealth of the many below because the further the top of the pyramid rises away from the base, then the more likely it will topple.

Focus on improving yourself then others will improve around you. Make the effort to listen to others and remember that there is logic behind what each and every one of us does. It can be skewed so much that it may not be obvious, but there is a reason to human nature and the behaviours we display. Each and every one of us is capable of great things so we must encourage and help each other because if we don't then there is truly no point to life.

The end

This book is a message to myself. At some point I've fallen into these traps. At some point in my life, I've been stuck in dead-ends thinking the worst and seemingly completely unable to get myself out of a rut. Whether they were financial problems, mental problems or problems forming relationships, I've felt a general uneasiness with life itself. The fear that life itself has no meaning has held me back for longer than I care to imagine.

Couple this with the woes of permanently being in debt and the continuous pursuit of punishing my body with poisons in the absurd hope that they were somehow the answer.

This is nothing new. These are normal problems that don't go away without looking into the cause and finding a solution. There are always solutions to problems and with enough application of effort, obstacles can be overcome.

This does not mean I now feel super-human and I am the perfect form of human, I just know I am better than I was. And each day I can try to be slightly better than the day before, and if I fall back into a former trap, I now understand where I am and I now have the tools to get out as quickly as I can.

I hope this has helped you and can continue to help you in some way. Thanks for reading.

Printed in Poland
by Amazon Fulfillment
Poland Sp. z o.o., Wrocław